Playing With

A play

Shaun Prendergast

Samuel French—London
www.samuelfrench-london.co.uk

© 2011 BY SHAUN PRENDERGAST

Rights of Performance by Amateurs are controlled by Samuel French Ltd, 52 Fitzroy Street, London W1T 5JR, and they, or their authorized agents, issue licences to amateurs on payment of a fee. **It is an infringement of the Copyright to give any performance or public reading of the play before the fee has been paid and the licence issued.**

The Royalty Fee indicated below is subject to contract and subject to variation at the sole discretion of Samuel French Ltd.

> Basic fee for each and every
> performance by amateurs   Code D
> in the British Isles

The Professional Rights in this play are controlled by MICHELINE STEINBERG ASSOCIATES, 104 GREAT PORTLAND STREET, LONDON W1W 6PE.

The publication of this play does not imply that it is necessarily available for performance by amateurs or professionals, either in the British Isles or Overseas. Amateurs and professionals considering a production are strongly advised in their own interests to apply to the appropriate agents for written consent before starting rehearsals or booking a theatre or hall.

The right of Shaun Prendergast to be identified as author of this work has been asserted by him in accordance with Section 77 of the Copyright, Designs and Patents Act 1988

ISBN 978 0 573 05260 3

Please see page iv for further copyright information

PLAYING WITH MY HEART

First performed by the Youth Theatre of Live Theatre Company, Newcastle upon Tyne, with the following cast of characters:

Ella	Lucy Heslop
Robbo	William Hardie
Paul	Jamie Tulip
Chantelle	Christina Whitehead
Lynn	Jenny Wilkinson
Zana	Jose Tchilombo
Domenic	Sebastien Fumoleau
Geordie (Mr Pride)	Darren Howie
Dad	Jamie Tulip
Yolande (Mrs Pride)	Jenny Wilkinson
Angel	Josephine Hepplewhite
Bernadette	Jenny Wilkinson
Mr Wood	Sebastien Fumoleau
Lucas Green Kid	Jamie Tulip

Director: Amy Golding
Designer: Molly Barrett
Production Manager: Drummond Orr
Assistant Director: Jon-Luke McKie
Costume Supervisor: Kate Eccles
Sound Design: Dave Flynn

COPYRIGHT INFORMATION
(See also page ii)

This play is fully protected under the Copyright Laws of the British Commonwealth of Nations, the United States of America and all countries of the Berne and Universal Copyright Conventions.

All rights, including Stage, Motion Picture, Radio, Television, Public Reading, and Translation into Foreign Languages, are strictly reserved.

No part of this publication may lawfully be reproduced in ANY form or by any means — photocopying, typescript, recording (including video-recording), manuscript, electronic, mechanical, or otherwise — or be transmitted or stored in a retrieval system, without prior permission.

Licences are issued subject to the understanding that it shall be made clear in all advertising matter that the audience will witness an amateur performance; that the names of the authors of the plays shall be included on all announcements and on all programmes; and that the integrity of the authors' work will be preserved.

The Royalty Fee is subject to contract and subject to variation at the sole discretion of Samuel French Ltd.

In Theatres or Halls seating Four Hundred or more the fee will be subject to negotiation.

In Territories Overseas the fee quoted in this Acting Edition may not apply. A fee will be quoted on application to our local authorized agent, or if there is no such agent, on application to Samuel French Ltd, London.

VIDEO-RECORDING OF AMATEUR PRODUCTIONS

Please note that the copyright laws governing video-recording are extremely complex and that it should not be assumed that any play may be video-recorded for *whatever purpose* without first obtaining the permission of the appropriate agents. The fact that a play is published by Samuel French Ltd does not indicate that video rights are available or that Samuel French Ltd controls such rights.

CHARACTERS

Ella
Robbo
Paul
Chantelle
Lynn
Zana
Domenic
Geordie (Mr Pride)
Dad
Yolande (Mrs Pride)
Angel
Bernadette
Mr Wood
Lucas Green Kid

The action takes place at the foot of the Angel of the North

Time—the present

PLAYING WITH MY HEART

The stage is dominated by the Angel of the North

A party is in progress. Everyone dances

Ella addresses the audience

Ella Now before we start, I've got to tell you I never liked angels, right, same as I never liked unicorns or fairies or any of that girl stuff, right? Just remember that. So the story starts like this....

The party breaks up and the dancers become a group of kids standing at the base of the Angel

... it's about a year ago and I'm with my mates.
Robbo It's a cold damp Friday afternoon ...
Paul ... after a tough week at school.
Chantelle ... and by rights we should be running out of the playground at Byatt Gardens.
Lynn ...yelling like maniacs...
Zana ...and getting stuck into the weekend ...
Domenic ... but we're not.
All (*annoyed*) No, we're not!
Ella No, we're stuck here, doing this rotten project, on the boring old Angel of the North.

They all blow a raspberry in the direction of the Angel

There's me right, I'm Ella, super-sports-woman, then there's ...
Robbo Robbo, I know more about music than anybody on the planet. I'm also nasty and mean and selfish and spiteful, so keep away.

Ella He talks rubbish. Then there's ...
Paul Paul. I'm Robbo's mate. I'm a bit shy.
Chantelle Next is Chantelle. I'm gorgeous. Worship me.
Lynn I'm Lynn. I'm the only sane one in the class. I keep them all in order.
Zana I'm Zana. 'Scuse me, I want to finish this drawing ...
Ella And finally ...
Domenic Domenic. Save the best till last. If you cut my leg off, there's star quality running through it like a stick of rock!
Ella Ignore him, he's all right really. And I'm Ella. I call them my mates but lately I haven't really been talking to any of them 'cos they've been so rotten since we lost the match ...

They all glower at her

... but anyway. We've been here all afternoon and we've eaten everything in our packed lunches, except Chantelle of course, who always says ...
Chantelle That's disgusting I'm not eating that.
Ella Even if it's something great like tomatoes which are my favourite she still says ...
Chantelle That's disgusting, I'm not eating that.
Domenic No wonder you're so skinny and get colds all the time.
Ella And there's nothing we don't know about the Angel, how tall it is, how wide ...
Chantelle How it was made ...
Zana How long it took ...
Robbo How much metal they wasted building the stupid thing ...
Zana How many people worked on it ...
Lynn How many cars drive past each day ...
Ella ... till facts about it were stuffed into my head like tissues and I felt like it was going to explode and start snowing angel thoughts everywhere! But Mr Pride wasn't satisfied, he wanted to look at our work.
Geordie Right let's see how you've wasted the afternoon hahahaha ...

Playing With My Heart

Robbo S'right, sir, it was wasted, education is all a waste, sir, it's pointless, sir. Like life.

Geordie You'll get nowhere with that attitude, Robbo.

Robbo Nothing wrong with my attitude, sir. It's the universe which is at fault.

Geordie Look at all this excellent work ...

The kids look bored at his jovial nature as they hand in their work

Lynn Sir. I've lost me ring, sir ...

Geordie Lovely drawing that, what Lynn?

Lynn 'Cept it's not mine it's me mam's and she's going to kill me 'cos she doesn't know I borrowed it.

Geordie Well, that's your own fault.

Lynn It kept slipping off but I found it. I must have dropped it.

Geordie Where did you have it last?

Lynn I was showing it to Paul and Robbo.

Paul It's really nice, sir.

Robbo Huh, just a bit of tat you mean.

Paul Eh, yeah, right, a bit of tat, like what Robbo said.

Lynn It was not tat, it was the last thing my dad bought me mam before he was killed!

Ella Lynn's dad was killed about three years ago. Car crash.

Lynn Tell them to stop saying it's tat, sir.

Geordie Boys.

Paul Sorry, Lynn.

Geordie Robbo.

Robbo Sorry, didn't mean to hurt your feelings.

Geordie Where did you last have this ring, Lynn?

Lynn Over there.

Geordie Well search there ...

Lynn She's going to go mad ...

Geordie It's your own fault, that's why there's a rule about not bringing other people's stuff to school.

Domenic Sir, sir ...

Geordie Domenic?

Domenic We're not at school we're on a trip, sir.

Geordie Very helpful observation, now be quiet.

Domenic You know what I wish, sir?

Geordie What?

Domenic I wish it was all trips and no school, sir. I wish school was on a bus, sir, and we just kept moving.

Geordie Well, yes, that would be nice, though a bit impractical. Couldn't improve your handwriting if the bus kept joggling about, could you? Now, what a wonderful and unique opportunity we've had to spend a day with the Angel ...

Lynn Not unique for Robbo, sir.

Domenic He lives in them flats.

Robbo If you can call it living.

Ella His big sister, she's twenty-two, she looks after them now, 'cos his dad left when Robbo was really little ...

Paul He can see the Angel from his bedroom window.

Robbo S'why I hate it, sir. S'just pathetic. Like everything else. Rubbish music ...

Ella By which he means anything that isn't Emo ...

Robbo School. Television. Governments.

Ella The funny thing about Robbo is, everybody else is always wrong except him. Nothing's ever his fault. It's always ...

Robbo People. The whole rotten human race.

Geordie Right, so the Angel does nothing for you, Robbo, but what did the rest of us learn?

Chantelle It's boring, sir, it's a big hunk of metal with arm ache. And it's got pigeons on it, I hate pigeons, I hate birds, they're disgusting and they spread poo, they're nearly as bad as boys. (*To Domenic*) Or *some* boys.

Domenic Whatever.

Chantelle Did you hear a mouse squeak?

Lynn No.

Domenic Whatever.

Ella Ignore them two. It's like a war, it's been going on for weeks. They used to be best mates till one day she said ...

Chantelle Helen Woods is just asking for it, you know what she called me the other day? Vain and cruel!

Playing With My Heart

Ella And Domenic said ...

Domenic Well you can be vain. And cruel.

Ella And that was it. From being best mates right, now she just ignores him.

Chantelle Sir, I hate this; it's all piddling dogs and pigeons and poo.

Geordie They're not pigeons, actually, they're magpies, you should know what a magpie is, eh. The symbol of United!

Chantelle And there's an old bloke with a dog and the dog's just done a huge one over there, sir, look under the Angel's wing, like she was pointing to the ground telling him where to do it!

Geordie That's enough about poo! Right class, pay attention now, we've learned some fascinating things, haven't we, like .... Paul?

Ella He always picks on Paul first.

Domenic ... 'cos last year on the school trip up a mountain Paul tripped up and banged his head.

Robbo ... and Mr Pride saved his life.

Lynn And Mr Pride never lets him forget it.

Ella He just points to his head when he asks Paul a question, like he's saying...

Geordie You'll answer this because I saved your life, boy.

Ella ... so Paul said.

Paul It was designed by Anthony Gormley.

Geordie Good, Paul! Robbo?

Robbo The wings are sixty metres off the ground ...

Geordie Very good.

Robbo Which means ...

Geordie There's more, go on Robbo, excellent ...

Robbo That if I dropped a penny from the wing and it landed on your head it would fall with such force it would split your head in two ... like a melon.

Geordie Ah.

Robbo emphasizes his point

Robbo Like a melon!

Geordie Well let's hope the angel isn't the type of bloke to throw his money around, eh? He he he! Geddit?

Lynn The angel's a girl.

Geordie I think you'll find it's based on the artist's body, and Anthony Gormley ...

Lynn It's a girl. Trust me.

Ella Sir, where's the bus?

Geordie Well, I was coming to that.

Domenic Should be here by now.

Lynn Sir, I've got to get home!

Ella I've got me trials for the county team tonight, if I don't get there I'm stuffed for a whole year ...

Geordie Yes, settle down, I'll explain what's happening, I have just had a phone call ...

Paul Sir, the bus is late ...

Geordie Yes Paul, I know that ...

Paul Sir, me mam's going to be worried.

Robbo She will, sir, she worries about him ...

Geordie I'm sure both your mothers will be fine...

An awkward silence among the kids. Robbo blushes furiously

What's wrong? What have I said? Robbo?

Robbo Nothing, sir.

Ella Robbo's mam's just gone to prison. For pinching money. But nobody said anything. Then Mr Pride remembered.

Geordie Right. Sorry.

Robbo Don't matter. Nothing matters.

Geordie Anyway, I have just this moment spoken to the bus company who say there's been a hold up on the bridge, so we might be stuck here for a while.

Ella How long?

Geordie At least an hour.

Ella Sir, sir, I need to get my dad to pick me up!!! Please, sir, it's an emergency!

Geordie 'Fraid not, Ella, there's a truck gone over on the bridge, nobody hurt thank goodness but they've closed it off, *and* there's been a breakdown in the tunnel, so everywhere's at a standstill.

Ella But this is a disaster! (*To the audience*) Then, when things couldn't get any worse, they did!
Geordie We're not the only school party stuck you know. Look over there, there's another mob, who is it? (*He looks, his face falls*) Oh. Oh no.

All look

All Oh no, it's ...
Ella Lucas Green!
All Lucas Green!
Ella Our deadliest enemies! Otherwise known as Pukus Green or Mucus Green.
Lynn Sir, we can't hang round with that lot.
Ella Even Mr Pride was looking sick now. And pretty soon, he looked even sicker, when the Lucas Green teacher came wandering over!

The actor playing Domenic pulls a jacket on and becomes Mr Wood

Mr Woods Geordie.
Geordie Brian.
Mr Woods Haven't seen you since the match.

Geordie smiles innocently

Geordie What match?
Ella But he knew what match.

All look at her, glowering

We all knew what match. The match where it was a draw so we had sudden death.

All look shocked

Penalties. And I took the penalty.

All look in anticipation

And kicked it as sweetly as I've ever kicked a penalty. Sent the keeper the wrong way and bent it up to the right hand corner...

In slow motion, the crowd watch with growing delight as the ball bends towards the goal

Till the wind caught it and it bounced off the cross bar.

All are horrified

And we lost.

All glower at her

And it was all my fault. They haven't forgiven me since.
Geordie Oh, that match, oh, ancient history, I'd forgotten that, too busy with other things to think about.
Mr Woods Not surprised, with your SAT results. See you, Geordie.

Geordie fumes

Geordie See you, Brian ...
Ella Sir, can I use your phone, please sir?
Robbo And me!
Paul And me!
Chantelle And me!
Lynn And me!
Zana And me!
Geordie Quiet!
Domenic And me, sir, I wanna use the phone, sir, I've got an auntie in California I haven't spoke to for ages.
Geordie Ha, Domenic, very funny.
Domenic I have, sir.
Ella Sir, me dad's got to come!
Geordie Quiet. Now, the school is ringing parents to let them know we'll be late but unless your dad's got a James Bond jet-pack he

won't be able to reach you. Well, Ella. Has your dad got a James Bond jet-pack?

Ella I was really tempted to say yes, I mean, it would be brilliant if he did, can you imagine it, where you off to, Dad?

Dad Just off down the shops for a pint of milk, love.

He jets off into the sky

Ella But he hasn't got a jet pack, he's got a Volkswagen Golf with a cracked wing mirror, so I said, "No sir".

Geordie I thought not!

Ella But I have to get back!

Geordie I'm sure you're not the only one.

Ella Sir, seriously sir, if we have to hang round with Lucas Green there's going to be trouble.

Geordie None of that talk now ...

Robbo She's right, sir.

Paul Sir, my mam's going to be really worried.

Chantelle I've got to get home, sir. And if I can't get home I'm going to get stressed and I don't do stressed 'cos it's bad for my complexion, but having Pukus Green over there is going to make things worse.

Geordie How exactly?

Chantelle 'Cos if I come out in a rash I'm going to kill someone. Someone from Lucas Pukus Mucus Green.

Ella As she said that, she said it good and loud, so loud it could be heard by Lucas Green. There was about the same number as us, but they were much much nastier.

The cast become the Lucas Green mob

Paul Bigger.
Lynn Rougher.
Robbo Tougher.
Chantelle Uglier.
Zana Thicker.
Domenic Quicker.

Geordie All right, all right, well look, can't you just play your Nintendo or something?
Robbo Sir, sir, that's a great idea! But me Nintendo's in my bag.
Geordie (*sighing, slowly*) Well where's your bag, Watson?
Robbo (*slowly*) On the bus, sir.
Ella Then it got worse! Suddenly one of the Lucas Green lasses looked over at Chantelle, right, pointed to her shoes, right ... and giggled to her mates ...!

Chantelle starts to explode

Then all her mates looked at Chantelle's shoes ...

The others notice

And they all giggled!

Chantelle begins a slow boil

Lynn Calm down, Chantelle.
Paul They're not worth it.
Robbo They're great shoes. Well, as great as shoes can be, they're only rotten shoes. But as rotten shoes go, they're great.
Ella But no-one insults Chantelle's shoes and gets away with it ... suddenly she burst like a spot!
Chantelle What you laughing at? Come here you fish-faced freak and I'll tear your throat out!
Geordie Chantelle, stop being silly. Right, sit down in a circle ...

Chorus of groans

Robbo Not this, sir ...
Zana We'll behave ...
Domenic Don't make us, sir ...
Geordie I'm aware there's always been a sporting rivalry between our school and them, but it's based on mutual respect.

Playing With My Heart

Ella Then one of the Lucas Green kids shouted.
Kid That's right, you lot listen to a story like bairns ... a story from your slap-headed teacher.
Ella Mr Pride went very still.
Kid Go on, baldy!
Ella Apart from a twitch ...
Zana And bulging eyes
Paul And a slight shake in the left knee.
Domenic I thought he was going to explode.
Robbo But instead he just said ...
Geordie ... plus the fact that we are a civilized school and they are a bunch of ... anyway, forget them. A good teacher can teach anywhere, so we'll just get on with our story circle.

Collective moan

Ella We hate this, right ...
Lynn It's Mr Pride's answer to getting involved with his class.
Zana He gets us all to sit round ...
Domenic And then one by one we have to tell something that's happened in our lives
Paul That made us sad ...
Zana Or happy ...
Paul Or whatever...
Zana He calls it being articulate about your emotions.
Domenic We call it sitting in a circle and whingeing.
Geordie Who's first? Come on? Anybody? Something about yourself.
Ella Sir, look, I'm sorry, but if I don't get home and I miss the trials I'll never get in the team and I'll have wasted all my training for a year, sir, and I'll probably die of a broken heart and it'll be your fault.
Domenic Will you cry at her funeral, sir?
Robbo Will you bring flowers?
Chantelle Wear a clean shirt?
Geordie Ha ha very funny. Right, Chantelle, you first.

Chantelle No.
Lucas Green Kid (*shouting*) Hey, look, it's slaphead and slapper!
Chantelle Right ...
Geordie Calm down, Chantelle.
Chantelle But ...

He restrains her, desperate

Geordie If no-one shares I suggest a sing-song!

All groan

All No, sir, not "Blaydon races" ...
Geordie "I went to Blaydon races, 'twas on the ninth of June ..."
Ella I couldn't stand it. Eventually I said, All right, I'll go first.
Geordie Good lass, Ella.
Ella So I said, sir, I'll tell you about a time I was really sad.
Chantelle Yawnsville, sir, this is so raw. Sir, when's the bus coming?
Geordie Quiet, Chantelle. Go on.
Ella We bought two goldfish and they got on really well, they were great, and I loved them, I loved them so much I thought I'd get another one, so I did, but when I put him in, the other two bullied him and a week later we found him floating in the water and we had to flush him down the loo.
Geordie Bullying is never right.
Chantelle Maybe the fish did something where he deserved to be bullied, sir; maybe he let down all the other fish in a football match.
Ella And everybody looked at me again. I wish I'd never said anything.
Geordie But thank you for sharing, Ella. Who's next, Robbo? Just tell us something that happened to you.
Robbo I was standing in this record store once and I'd asked and asked my ma for some money for a record but she didn't have any. But the gadgie in the store said I could listen for nothing so

I went in and just sat there and put the headphones on and it was like being in the best place I've ever been in my own head.
Geordie Solitude is very important in life, good for you. Someone else. Domenic?
Domenic Don't have anything to say.
Geordie Just the truth.
Domenic Thing is, sir, some people can't take the truth, even from somebody who just wants to be a friend. Sometimes they can't take it from someone who really likes them and thinks other people would like them if they got to know them.
Geordie Right, I think I got that. And are you talking about anyone in particular, one of your mates?
Domenic Don't have any mates. Permission to finish my drawing?
Geordie Yes ... Paul?

Nothing from Paul, who is lost, looking at Lynn. Mr Pride taps his head. Paul takes the hint

Paul Sir, I was shopping and I saw this comic, it's Megatron issue sixty-one, sir ...
Geordie Really?
Paul It's very rare.
Geordie I know quite a few comic collectors who'd give their right arm to own Megatron issue sixty-one.
Paul Anyway I said to Robbo I'm going to buy that, didn't I Robbo?
Robbo Yeah.
Paul And I've been washing cars and saving up but when I went to the shop to buy it, it had burnt down! But luckily the comic wasn't there and the owner's now selling it on the internet and I'm bidding for it. That's the other reason I want to get home, sir, so I can see if I've got it.
Geordie Well, you have to understand there's more important things in life than owning something.
Ella Mr Pride always listens to what we say and draws these little moral conclusions, it really gets on your wick.

Geordie Anyone else, Chantelle? Lynn?

Lynn Sir, it was my mam's birthday last week and we all made her a present right and we woke her up and we'd made breakfast and she was all asleep in bed, and as I was cuddling her, I looked, and on her dressing-table, all her make-up was there.

Geordie Right.

Lynn But it was all dusty. 'Cos she doesn't use it? She hasn't really used it since ... well, me dad bought her some lipstick, and she's still got it, so she hasn't used it since he died. And I thought that's what I'd really like to get her for her birthday. Someone to put make-up on for. I mean, I miss me dad. And it's not like I want someone to take his place. But me mam needs a cuddle. Everybody needs a cuddle.

Robbo Huh.

Lynn Even you.

Geordie Thank you, Lynn. Who's next?

Zana Me sir, I was in the cloakroom yesterday and I heard Lynn talking to her mate Sandra right, and Sandra said ——

Lynn Shut up, Zana!

Geordie Let him speak, Lynn.

Zana And Sandra said, "You fancy Paul, don't you?"

Lynn Shut up!

Zana And she said yes, sir!

Lynn I'm going to kill you, Zana, I never said it, I never!

Chantelle Paul, huh!

Zana Sir, he fancies her. Sir, he told us he did!

Ella And everybody looked at Paul. He didn't move he just stood there and went red. Not just red. More like a sort of a ...

Chantelle Tomatoey, scarletty ...

Robbo Bright, brilliant, crimsonny, carroty ——

Domenic — super-dooper red, red squared, red to the power of ten, a crashing red, like a brush of red paint or a brace of brave red soldiers or a big red balloon in bright red socks, a ——

Lynn — letter-box type of red, burning and blushing and ——

Ella — warming your hands on it type of a red, the kind of red you could post parcels in, or toast bread on kind of red. He was red.

Paul I went red. I'm going to kill you, Zana.

Lynn Me first.

Zana (*mocking*) So-reeeee!

Geordie What about you? Not something you heard about somebody else, but about you?

Zana Nothing to tell.

Geordie It's your turn.

Zana Me and me dad went shopping at the weekend and we had to buy clothes. When me mam was in the hospital she got him to take in a laptop and she did loads of shopping online so like I've got jeans and sweatshirts coming for ever 'cos she ordered them all. But we didn't know I'd get into Wheatley Bridge 'cos me SATs weren't till after the funeral. She wanted me to get in like. So we went to buy me blazer and ... (*He's upset*)

Geordie What happened?

Zana The man said me mam had phoned him from the hospital and ordered it, last year, but told him not to send it with the rest of the stuff in case I didn't get in. She didn't want to hurt me feelings. But she ordered it. 'Cos she thought I would get in. And I did.

Geordie Right. Thank you for that.

Ella looks at her watch

Ella Oh no ...

Geordie I'll phone the bus company again. See where the coach is.

Ella Too late for me, sir. I've missed the trials. That's a whole year's training wasted.

Geordie can't get a signal on his mobile

Geordie No signal. Everybody in the same boat. Right, Chantelle.

Chantelle No.

Geordie Come on.

Chantelle All right.

Geordie Yes?

Chantelle Well I had this dream.

Paul What was it about?

Chantelle It was about today. And in my dream we all got stuck here 'cos the coach broke down ...

Lynn Oh my God, sir, she's psychic, sir!

Geordie I don't suppose you dreamt what time the coach would turn up?

Chantelle No, sir.

Geordie So when did you have this dream? Last night?

Chantelle No, sir, just now when everybody was going on and on and being boring. I dreamt there was like a storm of boredom and there was thunderclouds in the sky ... and then lightning ... and a flash of lightning crashed across the sky. And hit the Angel, and she crumbled into dust ...

They all look at the Angel. Lightning and crash of thunder. The Angel wakes

Angel Huh, lightning doesn't frighten me, I laugh at lightning, hoy, ye, lightning, you're nowt!

Chantelle Sir, the Angel's talking!

The Angel climbs down, stretches

Angel Think this is impressive, you've seen nowt yet. Unlike me! I see everything from up here, I always have, since time began.

Robbo You were only built ten years ago.

Angel I've been here for ever, waiting to be built. From up there I can see everything ...

Chantelle What like?

The Byatt Gardens mob become everyone she's describing, ad libbing the dialogue

Angel Kids eating chips on Tynemouth beach, smelling of sea and salt and vinegar; beery blokes coming out the pub on a Saturday night, singing; a lonely lass picking flowers on the lonnen; the bright green grass of Saint James's Park, just growing and waiting for the next game. I see old girls grinning with a mouthful of crumbs in the Metro Centre, and an old bloke cradling a cabbage in his cracked hands as he fastens the gate on his allotment in North Shields. I see weary wifeys in Wallsend wishing the kids would hurry up and big blokes in Backworth queuing for petrol and shaking their heads. But listen, that's not all I see.

They return to being kids

I see you (*to Robbo*) scowling and trying to look mean and moody, and I see you caring about your mates underneath, and pretending not to. But you're not fooling me. I know under that Emo cut there's a lovely lad, even if you try to hide it by being —

Robbo Nasty and mean and selfish and spiteful —

Angel Listen. You feel guilty about your mam 'cos you think she pinched that money to buy your things. But she didn't. I saw her, day after day, losing all her money in the betting shop. Nowt you can do about that, and no matter how mean or spiteful you pretend to be, it'll never be your fault. Right?

Robbo Er ... right. (*He looks a bit shocked*) What else can you see?

Angel (*to Ella*) I see you practising your football to get out the house when your mam and dad are rowing, and I see you never give up. (*To Zana*) I see you crying over your class photo and telling your dad you're going to miss your mates, and I see all the mates you haven't met yet. And I see your dad. In a suit. (*To Lynn*) Meeting your ma. Wearing make-up.

Lynn and Zana digest this news

I see her (*indicating Lynn*) going red when she talks to him. (*To Paul*) And I see you asking your mam to go out and play, and her saying the roads are dangerous and you might get lost, and you getting lost in your comics instead. Incidentally, one day, you'll have the whole set.

Paul nods, dumbfounded

Paul The whole set?

Angel (*to Chantelle*) And I see you. Seeing your sister's face in the paper 'cos she's married to a footballer, and you getting jealous and being nasty to your friends, like him (*indicating Domenic*), who always stands up for you even when you're being horrible, which you are. Like when you took her ring.

Lynn You took my ring?

Chantelle Never.

Angel Did.

Chantelle Didn't.

Angel Hoy pet, I'm an angel, we only speak the truth. You took it, to annoy her, cause you're jealous of her.

Chantelle Sir, I didn't really have a dream, she's making this up. Tell her to stop.

Angel Once you ask an angel to speak, you have to shut up and listen. You're jealous 'cos people like Lynn. 'Cos she's nice. It's about time you stopped talking and started listening, (*indicating Domenic*) especially to him. Now you, you're going to be amazing, but you won't really realize your full potential till you get back from Kathmandu with Paul.

Paul Me?

Angel Both of you, in a few years time.

Domenic Kathmandu? Where's that?

Angel Better find out, hadn't you?

The Angel sniffs the night air

> Ah, the smell of Friday night. Now if you'll excuse me, I'm getting bored with it down here, I'm off to have a neb round, see what I can see. Nearly time for *Emmerdale* ... I can see it through that woman's window ...

The Angel ascends

Well? Haven't you lot got anything better to do than stare at an angel all day?

Chantelle produces the ring

Chantelle All right, I took your rotten ring. And I'm not giving it back.
Ella And then an amazing thing happened. It was Paul who saw it first.
Paul One magpie, black and white and high as a feather up on the angel's wing, nudged his mate with a squawk like a football rattle, then swept down from the left of the sky, swooped over and swiped the ring right out of Chantelle's claws!
Domenic She squeaks!
Chantelle I hate birds!
Domenic She shrieks!
Chantelle Disgusting!
Robbo Then the other magpie, and he sounded like he was swearing under his breath, dive bombed down and snatched the golden ring from the other one's gob!
Lynn Robbed him blind! Tackled it off him, back tracked in mid air, turned, sent him flying past and flew off!
Zana But who does he think he's kidding, the first bird's not beaten, look, he's bobbed up under, thundering through the air to thieve it back!
Paul Both birds rattle with the bitter battle.
Chantelle Every feather twitches!
Ella The ring switches!
Zana Gets swapped!
Paul Swapped again! Then dropped!

All watch it

Domenic ... all eyes on it as it shoots down out of the sky like a comet, down straight down, in a straight line, towards Mr Pride's bald head.

Ella Waiting.
Domenic Like a melon.
Ella To be split in two.

Robbo gives it emphasis

Robbo Like a melon.
Ella Nobody moved. Then, from nowhere, in slow motion, Paul grew ...
Zana Not red this time ...
Robbo Not even reddish.
Paul Just ready.
Ella He ran towards Mr Pride and rugby tackled him, just as the flying ring was going to fly through him ...

Paul tackles Geordie

All And Mr Pride is a big bloke!
Ella Threw him to one side.
Robbo As the ring embedded itself in the turf. Like a melon.
Ella Sir, sir, Paul saved your life, sir!
Robbo He's paid you back, sir!
Ella He doesn't owe you anything, sir.
Geordie They're right, Paul. Thank you.
Paul Anytime, Mr Pride. (*To Lynn*) There's your mam's ring back.

Everyone cheers as they move away from Chantelle, crowding round Paul and Lynn

Geordie 'Scuse me, I'll just make a quick phone call to the bus company see how things are ...
Ella And he wandered off while everybody's bigging Paul up.
Lynn You moved like a tiger!
Robbo You moved like a lion, man!
Paul Roaaaaaar!

Playing With My Heart

Domenic (*approaching Chantelle*) Hoy. You. Great story. You know, one day, I'm going to be famous, and you're going to regret not talking to me, because you'll have nothing to boast about. And you might as well talk to me, 'cos everybody else thinks you're horrible.
Chantelle Thanks.
Domenic But I don't. I think you're great and I really hate rowing with you. But it's up to you.

Pause

Chantelle Hey. I'm starving.
Domenic Want a fruit bar?
Chantelle Go on then.

They laugh, and eat

Ella And they became friends again. Which is all Domenic ever wanted ... Meanwhile, Mr Pride was on the phone, probably checking out the bus. Too late for me.
Geordie (*on the phone, away from the others*) Yolande, it's me.
Ella Oh, that's his wife. What's he ringing her for?
Yolande Hello love, is everything all right?
Geordie You know that comic I asked you to bid for me on eBay? Megatron Issue sixty-one? Forget it.
Yolande But you really wanted it. You said Megatron Issue sixty-one was all you needed to complete your collection.
Geordie Ay well ... it doesn't matter. Hey. I love you.
Yolande (*blushing*) Oh you daft ...
Geordie I'll be home as soon as I can.
Ella But just when we thought it was going to be all right, trouble brewed. From Pukus Green.

The Lucas Green kids gather

One of their lasses had wandered across and was drawing the Angel, and Zana, who's the best artist in the school ——

Lynn In the town.
Domenic In the county!
Chantelle In the country!
Paul In the world!
Robbo In the known universe including distant planets where snow is purple and sheep sing songs ——
Ella — wandered over to have a look.

Zana approaches the girl, Bernadette (the actress playing Lynn in a different blazer), who is standing sketching the Angel

Zana S'good.
Bernadette Thanks. Let's see yours then.

He shows her, his drawing

That's brilliant. I love the way you've done her wings!
Zana That's brilliant, the different shades of red and brown on his feet!
Bernadette Her feet. We've just had a big row in our class about whether she's a boy or a girl.
Zana My class has rows all the time. That's 'cos I'm in year six and we all get split up this year. Mr Pride says it unsettles us. He says it's 'cos friendships are breaking up.
Bernadette Tell me about it. Everybody just screams about it all the time, it's pathetic. I'm getting loads of hassle because I'm the only one in my school going to Wheatley Bridge. It's mad 'cos I don't know anybody there and they're all going to call me a chav and I'm going to hate it and all my old mates ... (*She looks bitterly at the Lucas Green party*) Behave like it was my choice.
Zana Same here. I'm the only one in my class going.
Bernadette Where?
Zana To Wheatley Bridge, same as you. I'm year six an' all.
Bernadette How do you feel about it?
Zana Great. See ... I like my mates, I get on with them fine ... but I don't feel I'm like them. I don't mean better, just ... different. I want different things. Like ... I hate football, which is like virtually

a crime in my school. Second, I like plays and theatre, which everybody thinks is posh. And it isn't. And lastly there's like a rule which says you have to think Newcastle is the centre of the universe and everything outside of it is rubbish. And I love Newcastle, it's great, but I've lived here all my life. So of course I want to leave. I told that to my mate Chantelle and she made out like I was a traitor, 'cos her idea of heaven is the Metro Centre.

Bernadette And what's your idea of heaven?

Zana Going to Mesopotamia, or Moscow, or Massachusetts, or ... anywhere.

Bernadette I feel exactly the same myself.

Ella It was all going so well, then a couple of the nastiest Pukus Green mob wandered over to Zana.

Lucas Green Kid Hoy. Ye. What ye deein' talking to a lass from wor school? What was he saying to you?

Zana It's a free country, I was just talking, it's not like it's against the law!

Lucas Green Kid Oh yeah?

Zana Oh yeah?

Lucas Green Kid Oh yeah?

Zana Oh yeah?

Lucas Green Kid Oh yeah?

Zana Oh yeah???

Geordie runs up

Geordie All right now, calm down you two, Mr Woods, Mr Woods.

Mr Woods Yes, Mr Pride?

Geordie I think the natives are getting restless.

Mr Woods Well, I'd suggest a football match but we all know we'd win, so ...

Geordie What did you say? That was a close match, remember, decided on penalties in heavy rain ...

Mr Woods Yeah, well, your side couldn't take the pressure, could they?

Geordie So what are you saying, you want a rematch?

Mr Woods Let's see, lads and lasses, do you fancy thrashing Byatt Gardens again?

Lucas Green kids cheer

Ella My lot were getting furious now, but when they lined up I felt a pang of worry.

Domenic We all did. Our lot were nice, normal, but standing opposite them the other team looked capable of ...

Lynn Ripping your head off ...

Paul Breaking your bones ...

Zana Chewing your ears to shreds ...

Lynn Pulling your feet off with their eyelashes ...

Ella Stuffing your mouth full of fluff from their belly buttons till you were sick.

Zana Then sitting on you till you flattened out like a Chinese pancake ready for hoisin sauce and shredded leek and duck.

Ella I knew then we were going to get murdered. And so, I think, did our lot, 'cos suddenly Robbo pointed and shouted with relief ...

Robbo The bus!

Ella And we all looked away. But Mr Pride and their teacher Mr Woods didn't look happy, in fact they both looked furious. Everyone looked at them.

Mr Woods Saved by the cavalry.

Geordie We'd beat you in a five minute kickabout even!

Mr Woods There's time for a penalty shootout.

Ella And he looked at Mucus Green and laughed.

Mr Wood laughs

And they looked at him and laughed.

Lucas Green laugh

And Mr Wood looked at Mr Pride and Mr Pride looked at Mr Wood, and Mr Wood said ——

Geordie You're on! With you and me in goal.

They act it out

Ella It was terrible. They took a penalty and Mr Pride saved it. We took a penalty and they saved it. It happened again, then they saved the third one. This next shot was it. If we could get a ball past their keeper our pride was saved, we could hold our heads high. If not, we were lower than a dung beetle ...

Domenic ... with no dung.

Mr Woods Well, you lot, last chance. Who fancies their chances against me?

Ella Geordie looked at Robbo, he shook his head.

Geordie Chantelle? Paul? No one ...

Ella He looked at them. They looked at their shoes. And then, horribly, they all looked at me!

Mr Woods She'll funk it.

Robbo No she won't, take the penalty, Ella!

Chantelle No she won't, choose somebody else! This is raw, sir, she's useless ...

Robbo Chantelle!

Chantelle Well, oh, all right, give her another chance then. Good luck, Ellie.

Zana Go on.

Paul Yeah. Look, from this angle you can see the angel between the goalposts. Aim straight for her heart!

Geordie It's down to you, Ellie.

Ella He placed the ball down.

All eyes on the ball

In the other goal, their teacher, Mr Woods, seemed like a huge daddy longlegs, all hands and legs and feet, filling the goal so much I could just see the bus inch his way past the traffic in the hole under his armpit. I licked my lips, paced out a run, turned, took a deep breath, looked at the heart of the Angel, ran and kicked ...

They act in out in slo mo

My heart sank. The ball curved just as I wanted it to, but I hadn't reckoned on how fast their teacher was. He even had time to smile to himself as he reached out a hand. It was right in the way of the ball, and I could see the big grin on his toothy face, and he did a little skip towards it and the Lucas Green lot cheered ...

They cheer

But then, an amazing thing happened. Their teacher put his foot right on the place where the old man's dog had done his business, and he slipped, and his hand dropped, and the ball sailed over it like a swallow through the sky and we all watched and as one we shouted ...

All (*shouting*) Goal!

Ella It was mental! And on the way back on the bus we sang along with Mr Pride.

All sing "Blaydon Races"

I haven't seen them much since. The ones in year six have left. Then last week, we met up at a party at Robbo's house.

Music

Chantelle Robbo, your mam looks well.

Robbo She's good, yeah.

Chantelle Still going down the bookies?

Robbo No she goes to these meetings now ... she seems calmer. How's your sister?

Chantelle Getting divorced. Who's that dancing with Zana?

Domenic Her name's Bernadette. She's in the same class as him at Wheatley Bridge.

Robbo Swot!

Lynn Oh, Wheatley Bridge boy, hiya ...

Playing With My Heart

Zana Yo ...

Lynn Sorry I'm late but we were swapping comics with Paul. Oh Zana, me mam says to tell your dad the concert starts at eight o'clock and if he's late this time he's finished!

Zana I'll make sure. He was only late last time 'cos I was sewing a button on his shirt. So you're still collecting the comics, Paul?

Paul I've now got the biggest collection in town I reckon.

Zana The county!

Lynn The country!

Chantelle The world!

Domenic The universe, even as far as the distant planets where cities are made from belly button fluff and frogs have nine legs and wear different coloured polo neck jumpers to match their moods ...

Ella How's your rehearsals going?

Domenic Brilliant. The teacher says I've got star potential, if I'd just learn to shut up and listen. How about you, Ella? Did you get into the county team yet?

Ella Yeah, first match next Tuesday.

Robbo Top! Gonna get some crisps. Chantelle?

Chantelle No, Domenic's got me into health food, crisps are so last week ...

Domenic Yeah, it's all smoothies in Hollywood. I'll have some juice though ... come on ... Ella? You coming?

Ella In a minute, I shouted back, but they couldn't hear me, 'cos Robbo's mum had put one of her old records on and all her girlfriends were dancing, and I looked out of the window and I thought ... maybe I do like angels after all.

All dance to "There Must Be An Angel" by the Eurythmics

THE END

FURNITURE AND PROPERTY LIST

On stage: Angel of the North statue
 Papers and pens (**Ella, Robbo, Paul, Chantelle, Lynn, Zana, Domenic**)

Personal: **Ella**: watch
 Chantelle: ring
 Geordie: mobile phone

LIGHTING PLOT

Property fittings required: nil

Exterior, the same scene throughout

To open: General exterior lighting

Cue 1   They all look at the **Angel**   (Page 16)
        Lightning

EFFECTS PLOT

Please read the following notice concerning the use of copyright material.

A licence issued by Samuel French Ltd to perform this play does not include permission to use the Incidental music specified in this copy. Where the place of performance is already licensed by the PERFORMING RIGHT SOCIETY a return of the music used must be made to them. If the place of performance is not so licensed then application should be made to the Performing Right Society, 29 Berners Street, London W1 (website: www.mcps-prs-alliance.co.uk).

A separate and additional licence from PHONOGRAPHIC PERFORMANCES LTD, 1 Upper James Street, London W1R 3HG (website: www.ppluk.com) is needed whenever commercial recordings are used.

Cue 1	To open *Party music*	(Page 1)
Cue 2	**Ella**: "So the story starts like this ..." *Fade music*	(Page 1)
Cue 3	They all look at the **Angel** *Crash of thunder*	(Page 16)
Cue 4	**Ella**: "... like angels after all." *Eurythmics: "There Must Be An Angel"*	(Page 27)

Printed by The Kingfisher Press, London NW10 7AS

A group of adolescents from Byatt Gardens School and their teacher are on an enforced field trip to Gateshead's iconic sculpture Angel of the North. With their coach delayed it isn't long before squabbles, misunderstandings, jealousies and antagonisms break out that require the Angel of the North to come down from her lofty height ... The arrival of their arch enemies from Lucas (or Pukus or Mucus) Green School with their jeers and taunts melds the group and when goaded into a football penalty shoot out, Ella gets the chance to redeem herself with a superb goal.

ISBN 0573052603